Pieces of the Heart

MIKE HASZTO

authorHOUSE®

AuthorHouse™
1663 Liberty Drive, Suite 200
Bloomington, IN 47403
www.authorhouse.com
Phone: 1-800-839-8640

First published by AuthorHouse 5/20/2008

ISBN: 978-1-4343-7926-9 (sc)

Library of Congress Control Number: 2008904432

Printed in the United States of America
Bloomington, Indiana

This book is printed on acid-free paper.

PIECES OF THE

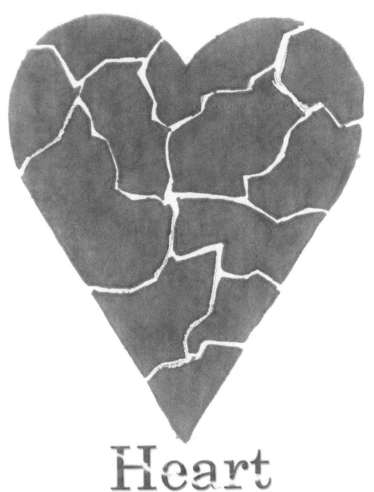

Heart

CONTENTS

FOREWORD...

Life is a proverbial rollercoaster. It really doesn't matter at what age, or at what stage of development. It really doesn't matter if one's perception is physically, mentally or spiritually.

Everyone is born with a heart. And the heart is in a constant growth pattern as it ages, picking up and discovering new feelings and new ways to deal with feelings.

Life is full of experiences, each and every one feeds into the heart. Each experience brings with it not just an overall feeling as a result, but adds different feelings that occur before the experience, during the experience, and after the experience, all of which helps to feed into the overall feelings of the experience.

Keeping all of this in mind, Pieces Of The Heart is a book full of poetic short stories concerning the equations of life.

Heart + Experiences = rollercoaster

As with life itself, this collection of writings is not organized or tabulated in any specific order. Life is an improvisization, and every genuine feeling that we as humans come across, is nothing more than an improvised reaction to any experience we encounter. One may argue that there are preplanned events that would bring out preplanned feelings, as in a wedding day for example. Sure, there is anticipation, and anxiety, nervousness, happiness, and hopefully euphoria. Many brides might admit to more feelings than those mentioned. Nonetheless, each one of those feelings that may be planned, may not be felt at all, depending on how the experience unfolds. Or those feelings may be felt in varying degrees. This because of the way the experience occurs, which really is improvised, even in the face of preplanning.

This collection has been assembled as a little therapy for the soul. It's generalizations will lead readers to a time where most have experienced something similar. It's details, sometimes graphic in nature, will bring out definite feelings, feelings felt not just on surface with a smile or a tear, but from the soul, where a smile will bring warmth, and a tear will bring a quiver.

I've always maintained that as a writer, the priority is to cause the reader to invoke the thought process into what has just been read. While anyone can write words on paper, only so many can actually express what they would like to say in those words.

From the simplistic "Heart" that opens the book, through "Misty Dreams", which closes this collection, there are many styles brought out, and many more 'Pieces of the Heart' unearthed.

Enjoy!

"Heart"

whole heart
half heart
pieces of the heart

encompass the emotions
warm the cockles
pick up the spirit
actually feel the warmth

unleash some passion
cage some rage
emote some fury
let go of the hostility

let depression escape
don't dwell on the sadness
wander through the grieving
don't turn anything into madness

pieces of the heart
half heart
whole heart

"USS Self-Discovery"

Go and tell Professor the journey has begun
It's time to pull the anchor up, start on the fun
We're heading out before the dawn will break
And where we'll go depends on what wind we take

      may be back again...

Go and tell the Captain our dreams have all set sail
We're on our way to anywhere now, won't accept to fail
There's none of us who want to stay where we are
All one team that will float amongst the star

      may be back again...

and we hear the voices that say
we're throwing it all away
their voices on the wind
saying we won't be back again

Go and tell the Captain we're all full speed ahead
We left our little shanties and our past of dread
Sadly, all of our dreams had run aground
Now there's not a person to keep us down...

      may be back again...

Go and tell the Captain our group will now take charge
We're united on a journey that's bigger than this barge
We're all in search of pieces of the heart
And we won't take a no on our discovery chart

going forward friend...
and we hear the voices that say
we're throwing it all away
their voices on the wind

saying we won't be back again

Go and tell the Captain that the tide is on the turn
Hit the storm of discovery, reached the point of no return
We can't wait to absorb all that we'll learn
All our questions answered, no need to yearn

won't be back again...

Go and get the Captain's log and tear the pages out
We totally unchartered now, we've reached what we're about
Taken a poll and none of us are left in any doubt
No need to turnabout...no need to turnabout...

won't go back again...

and we hear the voices that say
we're throwing it all away
their voices on the wind
saying we won't be back again
our time is nothing but a point
that runs along an infinite line
that has no beginning and no end
this trip was meant to be a joint

as we uncover and find

discoveries from within...

Go and tell the Captain we've reach our Newfoundland
We'll start our paradise with creations from at hand
We want to thank him for his time
Nothing left but move forward on our climb

      won't go back again...

Send a message to the ones back home
We've made it and are not alone
We've set up our futures and embrace what we have found
Just some self-discoveries of heart and sound

      and voices on the wind...

at night we still hear them say
we've thrown it all away
though we feel a brand new day
has got us up to stay...

Go and tell Professor that our dreams have all come true
Go and tell Professor that our findings will continue...
Go and tell Professor that is all about the heart...
Go and tell Professor that we'll never be apart...

"Red Alert"

Alert the world
    of a startling find
    that had been locked away
    in a simple mind...
    love...
    love...

Alert the world
    of a hybrid touch
    found to be
    never too much...
    laugh...
    laugh...

Alert the world
    of a changing rain
    once chilling yet now
    knows no pain...
    smile...
    smile...

Alert the world
    the end is near
    on the front of stress
    that once brought fears...
    peace...
    peace...

    love
    laugh
    smile
    peace

"Push The Envelop"

arise
a new dawning
a deep sensation
a quirky tingle
a bold thought
arise
and
create

create
candid ideas flow
caution let go
catch fleeting star
carnival from afar
create
change
motivate

motivate
mirror full cheer
minus the tears
marvel in mind
meeting all time
motivate
means
arise

arise to create
create to motivate
motivate to arise...

"Love Poetic"

in
a field
of green clover
amidst warm sunshine
and fluttering senses
true realization
materialized

it
became a
feeling so strong
the gods unleashed
all available angels
to harness
energy

the
absolute feel
was electric blue
immensely swallowing all
in its path
leaving only
love

love
in sight
in stark touch
in aromatic smell
in wondrous taste
in aura
love

"The Flow"

Pump...listen to the sounds...pump...sounds of silence...pump...
Pump...as they surrender...pump...to the rhythmic beat...pump...
Pump...of the emotion,,,pump,,,that can take one...pump...
Pump...higher...pump...faster...pump...passionate...pump...
Pump...intense...pump...focus...pump...more...pump
Pump...more...pump...more...pump...
Pump...more...pump...MORE...pump...
pump...whew...pump...ooooo...pump...
pump...whoa...pump...
pump...

zzzzzz...

"THE BANYAN TREE"

sitting under the banyan tree
absorbing the warm sunshine
enjoying the aromatics of the sea
welcoming the tranquil time

suddenly
out of nowhere
chills
tingles
envelop the scene

quickly
out of compare
thrills
mingles
living the dream

sitting under the banyan tree
in need of the warm sunshine
as my friend's pail of water soaks me
welcoming some exciting time

"Dream Number Three"

darkness
mystery
thoughts
history

pictures on the big screen
looking through a vail
moments frozen in time
can't identify detail

struggles
jumps
roll overs
bumps

much needed change of scene
awkward though clearing
baffling the mind
turns so endearing

palms
beach
you
peace

"MISSING"

The thought has crossed my mind
    full heart
    torn apart
    rebuild again
    find a friend
    emptiness here
    feel the fear
    letting in
    trust and then
    wanting to share
    feelings compare
    love in the air
    it's all there...

The thought has crossed my mind...again.

"MISSING (PART II)

How does one fill an empty heart
Need help in a direction to start

Over here...a definite fear
       which emotion
       of which ocean
       to be foundation
       in this proclamation
       standing here
       shedding a tear
       is it you
       what will do
       show me a sign
       outta time...

Over there...time to share
       how to start
       building a heart
       what to feel
       is it real
       happy or sad
       laugh or mad
       where to go
       end of rainbow
       show me a sign
       outta time...

How does one fill an empty heart...
I have a direction to start

Follow the ride...to get inside
                    leave behind
                    and open the mind
                    open arms
                    to feel the charms
                    must realize
                    twinkle in eyes
                    it's a steal
                    positive feel
                    go the mile
                    it's in the smile

How does one fill an empty heart?
Clocks running...time to start...
shhhhhh...it's one smile at a time...

"Spirit"

The car has just pulled out
 and the tears continued to flow
What took part was never in doubt
 but what will be revealed tomorrow...
Often , we measure life in time
 when experiences should be key
And while memories fade from the mind
 special journals keep history...

Dozens of events have occurred
 since upon the time we'd met
The bonds built all but spurred
 every feeling that's now left...
And with draining eyes now I sigh
 for our story has come to an end
So wondrous, one can see why I cry
 one could have never been a closer friend...

We tackled every challenge brought
 no matter the distance in miles
We conquered although we fought
 then laughed and smiled...
Two lonely souls coveting time together
 didn't care about the whats and hows
Two lonely souls connected forever
 though left with but one spirit now...

it took faith
it took courage
it took strength
it took persistence
        two hearts
        two souls
        two perspectives
        out of control
reaching out
supporting eyes
stirred and shaken
infinite skies

Dozens of experiences we shared
        and not one result was the same
Although our bias was quite unfair
        obsession was clearly our name...
But now the car has pulled out
        and I'm totally out of breath
Just can't believe all my doubt<
        over a true love's untimely death

        it'll take faith
        it'll take courage
        it'll take strength
        it'll take persistence...

and...many tissues...

"Mike"

Been awhile, you're on your own
Few months here, I'm living alone
What happened to you
And what will you do
I'm so glad to be free
Though I'm longing for company
Can you be there for again me
Just like back in history...

Been thinking of you, Mike
You know what I like
Come around like old times
We'll connect in rhymes
My eyes are open wide
For you to come on inside
And touch my very soul
For years it's been my goal...

We were such great friends
Spouses brought that to an end
But now with changing times
Opportunities are there to find
If you're feeling lost, too
And are struggling to continue
What do you say we try and do
Making one of me and you...

Been thinking of you, Mike
You know what I like
Come around and chat awhile
'Cause I need your smile
You could probably use one, too
Let me give that to you
And maybe we can feel a spark
That would rejuvenate our hearts...

Nothing but empty rooms now
All my flowers lost their blooms now
It's so hard to face the day
So many things I want to say
The nights go by so slow
My mind races through tomorrow
Your thoughts have been the show
I need my TLC to grow...

Been thinking of you, Mike
You know what I like
The door is so open wide
Come on and step inside
Longing to see you
Pick us up and continue
Longing to hold you
Tell me Mike what will you do...

"Urgency"

A little darkness and mystery
Remembering some of the history
Such an empty hole left
Love is completely in debt
Not sure why I bother to try
Still don't understand the whys
But I hold out for yesterdays
Where we were one in every way...

It must be the overnights
Nightmares and frights
Feeling dizzy and all
Suffocating is the call
Walls closing in on me
Can't handle this frenzy
What am I to do
I'm lost without you...

Have a full moon tonight
The werewolves are in sight
Putting the cloves around my neck
Can't believe I'm such a wreck
Every sound and creak I wince
Where is my perfect prince
I know you won't be coming
That doesn't stop me from running...

Sitting here inside my home
Sitting here all alone
Can't breathe at all

Suffocating is the call
Walls closing in on me
Can't handle this frenzy
What am I to do
I'm lost without you...

I find I dial your number
I text you while I slumber
I often call out your name
But emptiness wins the game
I cry and whine and scream
I'm so damn afraid to dream
I wish, I want and I yearn
For your love to quickly return...

I go through each day
Wanting you in every way
I turn to scope shadows then
In hopes of my misery to end
Oh no...here it comes again
Anxiety, panic comprehend
What am I to do
I'm lost without you...

so lost without you...
take my breath...
and close my eyes...
take me away...

"High Maintenance"

Hmmmm...last I knew...
        each person had a life of their own

So tell me why do you...
        make demands so arrogantly overblown

        remember the time of innocence
        where everything was so pure
        no thoughts, no ideas, no voice
        just natural actions for sure
        and along comes another person
        with thoughts, ideas and heart
        so incredible in beauty and smile
        personalities lead to a start
        but after the grace and intros
        honeymoon period has run out
        life is no longer innocent and pure
        it's high maintenance no doubt

Hmmmm...last I knew...
        each person had a life of their own

So tell me why do you...
        make demands so arrogantly overblown

enjoy the times together
and make sure you treasure
what it is that can be shared
and what that brings you pleasure
for at any given moment
the breath of life may end
and all that you'll have left
are arrogancies my friend
so get off the high horse you ride
and come back to reality
the need is to be down-to-earth
then your love will be safe with me...

Hmmmm...last I knew...
        each person had a life of their own

So tell me why do you...
        make demands so arrogantly overblown

Careful...it'll fade away...
        and that's a guarantee
No one controls this play...
        but I, myself, and me...

"CANVAS"

A parade whimsically marched down Main Street
Within full view of a mountainous seascape
The wizard guided a magical wand to meet
What was about to be just a moment too late

On the starry land with planets so oblique
The plains glowed like a stroke of the brush
This canvas was in no way for the mild or meek
But for the obsessors who are out of touch

Emotions floated on waves of blue and green
Passion was raised with the elevation of hello
One would have thought this was all a dream
Then an explosion of calm shattered the window

What could have possibly led to such a time
As the eagles soared with the island ducks
Could it be the thorny roses so blue out of line
Or the leprechauns merely running out of luck

Earthquake a quiver
Skin a shiver
Wave of passion
Skin a fashion
Colored hues
Me and you
Main Street
Canvas complete

"Confused"

Only takes a look
>and the heart skips a beat
>or the skin quivers in chill
>sudden stress to feel weak
>feeling mighty ill...

Only takes a word
>to capture the attention
>throw up the red flag
>need divine intervention
>secrets in the bag...

Only takes a touch
>the skin begins to crawl
>goosebumps on the rise
>hormones make the call
>twinkles in the eyes...

>>what's actual
>>what's perceived
>>what's given
>>what's received

One's thoughts
Perplexing personality
One's perceptions
Another's reality...

"Tease"

tease
squeeze
please
...me...

tease me
squeeze me
please me
...again...

you tease me
you squeeze me
you please me
...and again...

love the attention
love the smiles
love the brightness
it's love all worth while

no prevention
go the miles
sans frightness
always in style

realize
hypnotize
tantalize
...tease...

realize me
hypnotize me
tantalize me
...please...

you realize me
you hypnotize me
you tantalize me
...tease me...

"Please Me"

Please me every time
    she says
Thrilling how the time it goes
Can't feel it even though
    she has her ways

It's been plain to see
That even a lonely boy like me
Can partake in your cup of tea
I be
    in euphoria...

You came from nowhere
    and you shared your time
You caught me overwhelmed there
    and not just in mind
In spontaneous combustion it was we
    and afters it was still yearn
And in explosion we were to be
    and continued to learn

Please me every time
    she says
Exciting how the time we spend
Don't need another best friend
    she has her ways

It's been plain to feel
That a beach bum don't need to conceal
Much easier to just reveal
The deal
    in euphoria...

You opened your heart
     and you made my life worth living
Never since been apart
     and you lead with all your giving
You are the beacon in my eyes
     that leads me every way
I don't think you'll ever realize
     the full meaning of what I say

Please me every time
     she says
Full of meaning and such
Only takes but a touch
     she has her ways

It's been plain to be
Partners with her I see
Put us down in history
I'm really
     in euphoria...

"I Miss You"

We used to laugh
We used to hold hands
We used to walk together
Now we can't stand
We used to smile
We used to stare
Into each other's eyes
Now we can't bare
Here I sit to ponder
Why you're gone
There's no doubt now
I'll have to carry on

I miss you...
I miss you..

Wish I could change
Whatever sent you away
Haven't a clue
Why we're apart today
Wish you'd call
And talk this out
At least speak to me
So we'd leave no doubt
A simple email
To know you're there
Tell me you'll meet
I'll go anywhere

I miss you...
I miss you...

We used to talk
We used to kiss
We used to rub noses
It's that I miss
But I hold hope
And I hold our souls
And I yearn this day
For love to control
And I have no doubt
If you call today
We'll be together again
In every way...

I miss you..
I miss you...

"STRUGGLES"

Frustrations
Urgency
Pressure
Struggles

I want you here now...
I need you here now...
I'd die to be in your arms...now...

Emptiness
Burn
Loneliness
Struggles

I want you here now...
I need you here now...
I'd die to be in your arms...now...

Dizziness
Anxiety
Panic
Struggles

I want you here now...
I need you here now...
I'd die to be in your arms...now...

what i want
what i need
what i yearn
what i bleed
what i demand
what i scream
what i miss
what i dream

I want you here now...
I need you here now...
I'd die to be in your arms...now...

Temporary
Infinite
Intimate
Struggles

"You Are"

Like a mountainesque view
    so glowing and green
Or an Atlantic ocean so blue
    you are my dream...
Like a forest fire out of control
    so red and askew
With heat flaming intense
    my passions are you...

Like the moisture so warm
    of a sweet morning dew
Or the limitless clouds that form
    my thoughts are you...
Like the stars of mystery
    so infinite and bright
Or the dreams I dream so free
    you are my light...

    My passions are you...
    My thoughts are you...
    You are my dream...
    You are my light...

"DAYBREAK 2250 A.D."

The dawning of a new age;
> not just another orange sky below heaven,
> the stars fading as quick as the night,
> no darkness, no dreariness, no confusion.
Just the sound of imagination crackling in the air;
An atmosphere of amazement, of surprise;
The bright birth of a new sunshine floating
> through an open curtain into life,
> into a room containing only emotional love,
> such a love of each other and of life.
I turn to awaken in the sudden aura of gleam
> to find you there next to me.

And with all the creativity I can muster...
> I pray thanks that you are here, and,
> I turn to you caressing your skin,
> and gently whisper in your ear,
> I love you.

"TRIANGLE"

Whoever said having a third
Around for a little more than words
Would be a great idea to try...
When it's obvious that girlfriends
Cannot coexist together in the end
Leading to some great potential to die...

one
two
friend
do...
three
talk
feelings
start...

faces...
eyes...
blood...
cries...
jealousy
control
lost
souls...

All this nagging and stress
All this stalking and duress
The wanting to be in control
Don't waste our precious time
Reading in between the lines
You'll end up alone and cold...

Appreciate what is in front of you
And the opportunities will continue
Leading to happiness to say the least
Leave the triangle bullshit alone
And laugh and smile instead of moan
You'll find yourself in love's peace...

"Homeless Hope"

I am born this day
   sun beating down from a cold blue sky
   warmth felt from mom's fake fur
   and nourishment first sweet
   then barren and empty
I am two this day
   drops of rain my meal today
   cellophane surrounds cardboard walls
   my feet taped for the steps I take
   pigeons overhead making their calls
I am five this day
   the warmth of breath is all I have
   to keep these chilled bones alive
   unusually cold raw frost absorbs
   into an already numb skin of paste

      is this what life is about
      is this what i have to hope for
      a life of gypsy homelessness and doubt
      a life of tears, depression and more...

I am nine this day
   haven't seen a school or teacher
   the only books I see are for insulation
   I see tears forming on mom's eyes
   she is wilted as she cries
I am thirteen this day
   my body has been changing daily
   so fragile in mind and in body
   dinner but a bowl of soup and vitamin
   a quality birthday and lighted candle
I am eighteen this day
   a legal adult who can smile
   as someone has given me a job
   I won't disappoint mom anymore
   I certainly won't burden her as well

is this what life is about
is this what i have to hope for
a life of gypsy homelessness and doubt
a life of tears, depression and more...

I am twenty four this day
and have earned enough for a room
no more alley bathrooms for me
no more hose showers that chill
but mom has passed...I cry...as she turns forty...
She gave me everything
everything that a mom of sixteen could
everything that a mom homeless could
everything that a mom single and alone could
she protected me and showed me love
At twenty four this day
I vow to make my life more successful
using what mom taught me over the years
only degree I have is from the school of life
but it means everything to me now

i understand what life is about
i understand what i have to hope for
a life of hard work, struggles and doubt
a life of effort, energy and more...
i will not be beaten at any age
though the experiences have been rough
this stepping stone is just another stage
i will succeed and continue to be spiritually
tough...
thank you mom for not giving up on me
and for all your sacrifices...

"...LOVE..."

I know we always haven't seen eye to eye...
Fact is it was rare that we would agree
So in ways I can't explain the tears I cry
Especially with our kind of history...

There's a hole in my heart
Please don't say it's too late
Now is the best time to start
To fill that hole and celebrate
  ...love...

We've had our differences over the years
That type of relationship so parent/child
We've had our days of arguments and tears
You were authoritative and I was wild...

There's an emptiness in my heart
A puzzle so strong and great
It needs finished so over we may start
To understand each other and celebrate
  ...love...

    i know you're feeling weak
    i know it's about that time
    i know the clock is slowing its beat
    i know life is going blind

    hang on there for another minute
    for our very own peace of mind
    let's freeze this dream so we can both be in it
    and live this moment for all time<

Forgive me for being me
I didn't mean to fuss and fight

I've always had a respect you couldn't see
You've always been my beacon of light

Please watch over me , don't ever leave me be
I'm holding your hand through your final breaths
Mortality is so short, but you'll live in me spiritually
You'll be so alive in your new world as you leave here in death...

There's no finality in my heart
We are at peace together
I, too, close my eyes so we may start
Our new spiritual life forever

"Patchquilt"

Rain drizzling down the subway speakers
Static blaring stop after stop
Apprehension tossed about like marbles
Your look just another new-found tale

Climb those steps as daily symbols
To a discovery heightened by awe
Grab a pinch while possible to test waters
And pray the numbness shall never abandon

Just another quest into intense realism
To fatten up yet another overblown metaphor
Challenge the analogy with dueling verbiage
And arise scott free from the ashes

Such a passionate patchquilt of the heart
A vision here and several stitches there
Each another vibrant color of feeling
And each chockful of energy and meaning

Patch me up...

"URBAN LEGEND"

Urban legend
Intimidating setting
Anger loaded
Realism exploded

Pop
Pop

On the floor
Innocent no more
Out of breath
Urban death

Procession in black
Life off track
Lack of respect
All about neglect

Now playing at a city near you...

"BETRAYAL"

I see the look in your eyes
Just lost your best friend
It'll take long distance to reach you
I'm getting busy signals time and again...

In a parallel universe you say
Not in a happy place I see
So frustrating when you're betrayed
Back in a shell is where you'll be

      the adrenaline is understood
      the feeling of being upset
      change direction if only you could
      betrayal you just don't forget

Someone said there's a thin line
Between love and hate
Exponate the relationship another level
And feel what resonates

Must be some powerful jealousy
Combined with some intense hate
To want to execute a person friendly
And destroy a trust so great...

sense
anger
frustration
suffocation
depression

sense
rawness
insert
hurt
regression

betrayal

"Pieces of the Heart"

How I wish this was a perfect world
     in a perfect universe
Where rainbows would fill a sunny sky
     where reality could never be worse

Where each emotion had meaning
     each feeling would redeem
Where all the beautiful creative visions
     would grow into reality from dreams

Come and feel with me:
     a look
     a wink
     love is our drink

     holding hands
     warm feel
     peace is our meal

     frustration
     some tears
     challenges are what we hear

     depression
     being alone
     obstacles in our home

     anger confusion
     being afraid
     feelings are what we've made

hugs
and a kiss
feelings we don't want to miss

How I wish this was a perfect world...
How I wish...
       ...this was a perfect world...

"Memories"

Years come and go through life
Experiences mold one so right
Snapshots are character personified
Results were efforts true and tried

Childhood messes and mistakes
Adolescence put on the brakes
High school proms and graduations
College parties and adult education

Socialite the major again and again
Quality not quantity measurement of friends
Athletic events and a posture so proud
Slow dances with Stairway cranked loud

Vacations taken with palm by the sea
Atlantic Ocean up to the Statue of Liberty
All about pictures and funny video
Remember yesterday, plan for tomorrow

Marriage with an entree of sweet romance
Reception hit was twice the chicken dance
Births of family were five times aplenty
Chronicling all their events up to twenty

Cycles of life always going round and round
Always dealing laughs, always the biggest clowns
Infinite memories, always in touch with a few
Infinite storage with so much room to continue

The bottom line in most memories
Is actually the doing of the history
Family, friends, or whether alone
To close your eyes and always feel home
Keep those experiences fresh and sharp
And keep those feelings close to the heart
Doesn't matter the day, year or age
Just reminisce through another stage

And let those tears swell...
It's the eyes that always tell...
Let the heart skip a beat
Relive the passion, relive the heat
Don't be afraid to spend the time
Tell the family feelings in rhyme
One last bit of vision finally
Always smile when living the memories...

"CRY"

birth	death
nurturing	stagnant
teach develop	cold alone
independence	dependence
confidence	fear
experience time	experience life
right or wrong	left or right
confess	secrets

make your life
yearn with passion
urgency in fashion
create it all
live while you can...

one day the luck runs out
you get the call
you feel the fall
it's a long way down
from health and sanity

one day you're here
the next you're there
one moment you smile
one moment it's wild
one moment all is gone

loss of spouse
loss of family
loss of friend
loss of me
cry

"Wild"

Shall we walk
    wild
and cruise by the junipers
    as we
gently hold hands and
    whisper
each others thoughts and
    dreams
into our personal
    paradise
filled with loving
    desires
that only you and I
    wildly
may discover and share...
Shall we converse
    wild
and open up the doors
    boldly
to let in each
    hope
and prayer and
    passion
that swallows us
    whole
and commit to what
    intense
euphoria may hold
    wildly
for our infinite future...

Wildly visionary...
Instinctually wild...

"ABUSED SOAP"

I was born, yes, born,
    not hatched, nor caught,
    on a wet, dreary friday morn.
And upon my delivery into this new land
    I could feel love and warmth.
As my existence went on into days,
    then months, not to forget weeks,
    I could feel poor, yet loving parents.
My rookie year into this vast new existence
    proved confident, even exciting,
    until the bottom fell out.
Yes, my enthusiastic experiences dwindled
    into a sullen darkness.
My youthful opening suddenly
    had fallen into obliqueness.
The bottom line: the ceasement of attention.
For my baby brother had been born,
    ah yes, the family angel.
    Oh, how he could do no wrong.
My parent's swollen smiles and cheeriness
    dwelled upon my new relative.
    And, why not, for he had the good looks.
While he played joyously with his toys,
    I got screamed at for even the sunshine.
Imagine, a one year old, getting yelled at!
It seemed as though I was a devil,
    that I was purely satanic.
Imagine, a one year old, already turned criminal,
    and serving punishment in my crib.
Oddly enough, a new addition came the next year,
    a beautiful sister,
    yet, my now year old brother still captured
    the coveted crown of attention.
    Yes, my brother the angel.
Still, my sis deserved and received

all the loving she needed.
Yet, I'm now two years old,
        feeling as though I'm twenty
        and moving out of the house already.
However, when my next sis entered
        this sensational world, a year later,
        I was very much used to being alone,
        being snubbed.
If my brother wanted anything,
        he'd receive it.
The only thing I received was "no".
At four years old, I entered a world
        what seemed like death.
        I talk of my first bonafide spanking.
        I couldn't believe it, I had some attention.
        My crime was coloring the walls with crayons...
        my brother's crayons...the angel.
        Actually, he was the one who colored the walls.
        Then he told mom I did it.
        Such an angel.
At five, I was physically abused frequently
        for I was an adventurer,
        and I discovered wrong things.
        That was the extent of existence in communications.
My brother and sister, twins, arrived when I was five.
        Gee, the highlight of my life then
        was spilling milk and getting
        the whole container poured over my head.
        I actually enjoyed the ritual,
        however, my family was poor,
        and after using up countless gallons of milk,
        I was just smacked in the face.
To keep myself from total withdrawl,
        I taught myself soccer and baseball
        when I reached six.
        I also had made one friend in first grade,
        who played G.I. Joe with me.

That is, until my Joe lost an arm,
and my parents refused to purchase another.
One G.I. Joe lost on the battlefield,
and one sensitive child losing a war,
a war concerning the will to survive.
But, I mustn't exaggerate.
Honestly, my parents came to see
my athletic events, baseball and soccer,
however, they seemed pleased only when
my brother did well,
my brother the angel,
and they didn't seem to care about me,
although I usually did much better.
I never thought I'd reach double figures in age,
so I fooled myself come my tenth birthday.
My parents were nice to me,
unfortunately, though, my birthday
occupied the very day prior to my dad's.
So, I got cheated on my own cake,
and I lost the one hope of a day that
I might receive some notice.
Things remained quiet in my life for some time,
in fact, until puberty.
I could guess that I was in for something bad,
for I wasn't ever noted in about three years.
But, to make a soap opera even longer,
I was disowned by my mom in the fourth grade
for being thickheaded.
And to make things worse,
my parents talked to my brother about puberty
and love and sex.
They never said anything to me,
it seemed as though they figured
I had already engaged myself in some sort of
that evil stuff.
How wrong they were,
for I didn't know the difference

between male and female,
        except maybe long hair on girls,
        and I frankly didn't care.
Every time I attempted to inquire,
        I would receive answers like
        "when you get much older".
        How much older could I get?
My dad kept me in the household during trying times.
He kept me in the family unit,
        while mom shrieked alienation from me.
        She wanted to exile me,
        hoping several hundred spiders
        would carry me off to websville.
        Alas, her dreams never came true.
        I'm sorry, mom.
High school showed me they still cared for me,
        yet still no notice for any achievements.
        I could sense a bad freshman year,
        for my mom wouldn't even attend my
        grammar school graduation.
        Imagine that.
Freshman year matured me immensely.
        I knew what it was like to be alone,
        to have self-discipline in sports,
        and to attempt suicide.
I found a friend who was very much like me,
        withdrawn and alone,
        and, to this day, we're still best friends.
We showed each other praise
        for our athletic achievements
        me; soccer, track, and baseball,
        him; track, all year long.
I was pretty intelligent my whole school career,
        all A's,
        yet I received crucifixion for not
        studying twenty-four hours a day.
        Of course, my brother received A's too,

and he was praised because he did study 24 hours a day.
Sophomore, junior, and senior years,
      I almost found out what it's like
      to know a girl, yes one girl.
      However, my parents killed my maturing experience
      saying I was too young, and,
      too occupied in school and sports.
      I disagreed with them, but,
      as usual, they prevailed.
Dreariness seems to play a major role in my life,
      along with the monsoon rains.
      It rained on the day I was born,
      yes, born,
      on the day I graduated kindergarten,
      on the afternoon I graduated grade school,
      on the morning I received my All-American status in soccer,
      and on my graduation day from high school.
      Yes, I actually made it through high school,
      can you believe it?
I graduated with honors,
      yet my parents found something to put me down for.
I received scholarship offers from colleges,
      yet again I was criticized,
      for I never got a four year free ride.
      They blamed me,
      and being brainwashed with shame all my life,
      I blamed myself.
After heated arguments and threats,
      I left for Akron, Ohio,
      for what seemed like even more obscurity.
My first year trademarked my eighteen year existence
      as all went wrong.
      To let you in on a secret,
      Ziggy is my middle name.
      Honestly.
      Yet, he had one thing I didn't have,
      at least then,

a loving dog.
I got lost in hum-drum Akron,
with the only excitement I got,
if you can call it excitement,
was the poor taste of rumors circulating campus.
Sure, it hurt me,
I reached the new low I never thought I could.
I was below bottom.
I did receive some signs of attention,
and friendship,
but it didn't outshine the many clouds
in my reality.
I wonder why.
I became diseased during my premier year,
again contemplating the strength of survival.
Still, I played baseball, did well,
yet received no praise for it.
So, I went into seclusion over the summer of '78
and returned for a dynamite
second campaign.
With disease still lingering upon me,
I met the highlight of my life.
A female,
a beautiful female,
she even talked to me,
and she actually smiled.
We grew together quickly,
and she put up with me somehow,
I was such a charity case I guess,
but that was something I never thought could happen.
She showed me love,
yes, love,
an emotion I rarely felt prior to meeting her.
I was in love,
I loved her.
My life has been up since then,
for, at least, the most part.

I feel the need to be.
Yet, I feel depressed still about
        dumb, unnatural things
        like attention.
Oh well, I guess I still have
        a long way to go.
And, if you ever read this, my love,
        thank you for everything.
        I love you.

"ABUSED SOAP (STILL LATHERING)"

I still breathe, yes, breathe,
    with my own lungs,
    on my own,
    without the aid of a machine,
    or any modern drugs...
    yeah, I still breathe.
It's been sort of a minor miracle
    that a life so distinctly abused
    in whatever ways possible
    continues to this day...
Ooops, guess you can stop right here.
I gave away the ending.
Old Murphy here just can't keep secrets
    while telling stories...
    such a curse.
After telling the tale of Ziggy
    and the childhood that wasn't
    storybook material,
    the next stages mined the
    very same vein in my tale of life.
The love professed to a female,
    my goddess,
    lasted about the time it takes
    to boil an egg.
    Okay, maybe a tad bit shorter.
This digression can be titled something like
    let's spend a weekend with
    the in-laws, and catch her cheating.
    Which I did.
    Which she did.
    Which I did.
    Then, in the true style of the character
    in the Simon and Garfunkel song "America",
    I hitchhike back to college,
    over fifty miles,

and interstate roads,
    again pondering philosophically
    just why do I continue to live...
Earthshattering.
Truly.
But for those people who have never felt
    the simple but nonetheless intense
    stings and scars left upon you
    by such a humbling existence,
    you really don't understand.
By all expert estimates,
    that leaves 98% of you in that category.
So, maybe 2% of you can feel the pain...
    and go on.
    Go on like me...
    an aberration of sorts...
    a missing link to neither a past or future
    but to a present where souls cry and moan
    and wail...
    and where the meaning of soothe
    just doesn't exist.
For the next six months, I was, well, deep.
    Deep in seclusion.
    Deep in thought.
    Deep in depression.
    Real depression.
    The kind where you don't initiate anything.
    The kind that you don't recognize anything.
    The kind that can let twenty years go by
    and absolutely nothing has changed,
    except the jersey number I wear
    signifying my age.
Alas, twenty years did not go by.
Year three in Akron...what can I say?
    Soccer...baseball...well, no baseball.
    Running in a thunderstorm
    on concrete with flip-flops

leads to hydroplaning
which leads to a somewhat spectacular
flight in mid air
and as gravity would have it,
scrape my foot and dislocate some toes
and well...feel more pain.
Actually, that had nothing to do with baseball...
just another Akron accident, not waiting to happen,
but did actually happen.
First and only time I've seen toes sideways out of my foot.
Crazy.
College soccer took care
of whatever baseball dreams
were left.
Injuries suck.
There's no better description than simplicity for injuries.
Gotta love my luck.
Let's revisit the rain theory...
it rained the day I caught her cheating...
it rained throughout the hitch hike...
it rained for the dislocations...
it rained the game I was permanently
left with a bad knee in Indiana...
hmmm...yet I love thunderstorms...
makes me feel all warm and chummy.
Interesting.
So mister big man on campus jock had to
change course in life again.
Nothing huge though.
Just lost the one thing that meant so much,
that kept me alive all these years,
that was, indeed, me.
That gift of athleticism.
I'd say the gift of attracting women,
but who am I kidding?
So I turn back to a budding interest I had
since the days of euphoria

living in the house with a satan (mom)
and an angel (brother)...
that interest was...radio.
Radio led to music
Which led to lyrics
Which led to Olivia Newton-John...oooops...
The lyrics led to personal development in writing,
which fed right into expressing thoughts,
not that anyone cared.
Writing.
A gift.
Something no one can take from me.
I can lose so many things...
I have lost so many things...
but the gift of writing
just keeps on giving...
So, once again, I wrote...and I wrote...
and wrote some more...
And to this day, I still write.
But again, I get ahead of myself.
Will somebody shut me up please?
Then again, I suspect, there's only 2% of anyone
that began reading this to still be around...
and 2% of nothing...
is still nothing...
or in this case, no one.
And no one wants to hear of all the misery
and lost soul stories that can be shared,
so let's all take a moment and
shed a tear in our beer,
so we can all move on.
Great.
Year three in college brought
another female that brought meaning
to love,
to life.
I thought I'd scare her away like the first,

because true to life,
I blamed myself for her cheating on me.
And I blamed myself for catching her cheat.
And so on...
Anyway, as the abused soap still lathers,
          she is still with me...
          five kids and twenty five years later...
          all in some capacity
          somewhat intact.
The bouts of childhood are still very real,
          and still decide to visit quite frequently.
          Amazing how the things we all
          grow up with still come back
          and try to thrive
          in a present environment.
Amazing is that the other half of me
          has stuck by me
          to ensure those childhood
          experiences don't creep
          into parenthood.
          The scars are still so fresh and so deep
          that I really didn't need alot of help,
          because I knew that in most cases
          the opposite of what I experienced
          was the right answer.
And, the kids have turned out fine.
At last count, as I check the scoreboard,
          only three of seven kids in my family
          still talk with satan.
          the angel doesn't.
          Why?
          Who knows...maybe it has some
          religious ramifications...
          All five of mine are safe...
          and are somewhat successful...
          and the lines of communication
          are wide open.

I admit I miss all the hullabaloo
        that was once my chaotic life.
My life has meaning and purpose...
        even though I still have long bouts
        of loneliness
        and pain,
        and for some reason,
        I'm always cold.
        But rarely my feelings are cold.
        Just buried.
        Like a treasure.
        They were found twenty five years ago
        by a special woman.
        They can be, and will be found again.
        And again.
        And again.
Someday, you will read about the last twenty five years.
Maybe...
Perhaps...
It's been an experience...
        an infinite rollercoaster,
        with no track...
        sometimes a magic carpet ride,
        and sometimes a tragedy in the making.
I used to hate life.

I used to despise life.
I wanted to end life.
Badly.
I'm so happy to be here.
With all the scars
With all the past
And with all the baggage.
It's time to lather up some happy memories...
Pass the soap.

"Appreciation"

Cultivate
You look so awesome tonight
That my heart keeps skipping a beat
Don't know if I can stay in control...
Just to walk beside you
And hold your tender hand
Your beauty touches into my soul...

Captivate
Your eyes hold a conversation
With mine at every glance
And my blood keeps pumping so fast...
The looks that you emote
Send chills through my spine
It proves these feelings will forever last...

Radiate
Just what are your secrets
That you command such attention
And how do you eternally glow...
I'm infinitely proud just to be with you
I'm so humbled with your company
You are the gold at the end of our rainbow...

Appreciate
Whatever time we spend together
All those moments I cherish
Your love just eternally fills my heart
May those times become frozen
So our love may last forever
There's nothing that could keep us apart...

Let me whisper...
Thank you..
I love you...

"Just Say It"

Waffling amongst a mess of hesitation
Salt so thick from all the perspiration
Loosen the twitchy collar around that neck
Quickly now for all around are wrecks
Deep breath in with calm yet verve
Feel the urgency and feel the nerve
Shyness makes speech so complex to say
The moment though is fluttering away...

       hold the hand
       look into the eyes
       touch the soul
          so gently
       whisper now...
       i love you

"Missing Him"

Dinner table conversation heard in the air
Everyone's gathered around competitive compare
Usual fights over food and success
It's the present that's created this mess
Light flickers a moment, then settles in dim
Back to reality has me missing him
As I stare across my plate to see another
Yet it's so empty, as my heart, I wonder
The grieving never ends as much as I try
The appetite fades as tears swell my eyes
So much for dinner and the conversation I hear
So much to dream and have reality so clear
I wish he could come back for my heart bleeds
I wish he was here for I am in need

"WHERE"

Once here and now gone...but where
Crystalization has become a focused view
Fore-go the prisms as optical illusions
Hard cold facts place you at the scene...
And such a scene:
     spending time
     developing in rhyme
     trading smiles
     all the while
     laughing and playing
     planning and praying
So...how about an explanation
Graft theory and philosophy and fantasy
With a bit of homebrew realism stark
Tears not necessary, but peace and love are...

     the question is where?
     as in where...are...you?

No game of hide and seek shall rule
Moreover holding breath only gets me blue
Chapters have passed and glory lived
Though realization comes unfulfilled
The fun comes from sharing life every way
But your lifelong gift received was eternal...
     ...alone...yes...
     ...empty...yes...
     ...but the gift was...questions...

"Dainty Custard"

Radiant quirks grasp scratchy humanity
Horizontal flashbacks flavor unsettling moods
Detain these designated secluded secrets
Plug them into integrated groupings under palm
Cover the distant views with invisible bounds
Dismiss pathetic passages as unknowingly ignorant
For innocence strikes an exciting chord of voice
And euphoria shall be felt by a protective all within

"DAINTY CUSTARD (THE FEAST)"

The blind magistrates through a process of touch
As darkness shreds any mystery of what will be
Passable partners insist interest envelops such
And what unfolds will leave no small fantasy
Melange melancholy were not issued invitations
For what involved a tasty feast of connivance
That evolved in conception without limitations
With the properly trained of mind reaching chance

      taste oh taste
      upon these feast
      and leave nothing to the mind
      relish not least
      fantasies to last a lifetime

"Dainty Custard (Dessert)"

Irresistible restlessness stroked away kind
A flair for energy has seceded succinctly
Groups released now again frozen in time
Brought together for this purpose distinctly
Premium recruitment lay pleasurably still
As the bewitching birth discovers dalliance
Such an occasion of everyone's free will
With an encore of a multi-greedy slow dance
       all with a lightness of cream
       that baffles the mind so aimlessly
       occupies recreation of a tasty dream
       elevate energy for another fantasy...

"DAINTY CUSTARD (FOR AFTERS)"

Celebration of affairs now long extinct
Breathtaking excitement has ripened past
Time is for all now to go back to instincts
Rekindle consummate feelings to last
Take another lick...feast on another taste
There's still experience enough to go around
Don't take for granted and certainly do not waste
These sailing emotions that have come aground
       lovely chocolate fondue
       earns tongue lashing of free
       a pass to stringently continue
       to share the custard of three
       whip...whipped cream and some
       socialize 'til the custard fades done...

"Fainty Mustard"

All have opportunity to witness what is ahead
As all have same chance to experience behind
Consider the peripheral and a keen awareness
And one reaches what is known as potential
Emotions do not lie with surface scratchings
For that shall be known as mustard of the faint
Rather seek out and dig uncharted land
And will the passion for the custard of the daint
Again do not belie what may be social calling
Certainly do not yield for society conscience
Stand up and discover that for what is one's reality
And leave mustards of the faint for the same of heart

        arise and experience
        seek and discover
        mighty sequoia
        growth and deliver...
        with the breezes of life
        better to stand tall and shiver
        than to weep within
        and hide and cover

"Saintly Trustard"

Painting a pallid canvas from a vibrant palette
Nestled in new-found wonder deep within hue
A social misfit reached for a parallel mistake
With irrepressible interpretation utterly limitless
Gesturing implicitly with tongue in moist cheek
The artist screamed for organization of tonality
Still seething yet searching for perspective perfection
And suddenly the pallidness grew with passion
      fire lit the canvas with unyielding heat
      that implored a never achieved intensity

With the touch of a chord finally in syncopation
Orioles and bluebirds bled their vibrancy in harmony
As brick upon brick castled in solemn togetherness
Until all rainbows choreographed to but a single one

Looking around for awareness instinctually
A minuscule sachet emitted a sweet odor
And for one brief moment frozen years ago
The artist relived his art, his dream, his life
Opening his eyes mysteriously appeared to be
What has caused all the chaos dominated sacredly
Triumphantly another masterpiece of epic proportions
Brought out a creative energy leading to explosions
Of light, of paint, of color, and of dreams...
and he named it...

You...

"SIMPLICITY"

twas but a jounce
a sudden prime shake
that left a soulful heart
in its clarion wake
a flash of brightness led
to quite an awakening of awe
reminiscent of sunrise aglow
just a silhouette i saw

soft brown orbs enveloped
with a hint of sparkling green
she smiled a snowy twinkle
just first act of my life's dream
another stir brought a quick chill
so overwhelming down the spine
a graceful touch of the lips
and i was completely lost in time

an abundance of pleasure
combined with wild combinations
flowers and clouds of rapture
and a few undefined sensations
started with just a jounce
and soon it was a lost control
broken down in total simplicity
it was when hearts met souls

"Hearsay"

nothing like a good ole tale
to put everyone in an uproar
always marked pass or fail
never know what's in store
did ya hear...did ya hear
it was he...it was she...
afterwards crocodile tears
then on to another story...

ever examine involved hurt
from all concerned parties there
what was an innocent flirt
evolved into hearsay to share
this ruins lives every time
people left in cross-eyed awe
doesn't matter lost minds
always what they allegedly saw

whisper...whisper...whisper...
did you hear about...
whisper...whisper...whisper...
it's true no doubt...
whisper...whisper...whisper
these things never pass
whisper...whisper...whisper...
try to rebuild from ash

lost again to hearsay
nobody seems to care
no defense anyway
the truth why share
just assholes who cause trouble
through jealousy and hate
speaking in tongues double
purpose to permanently berate...

cry...all of you...painful cultivate
die...all of you...a suffering fate...

"Voices of the Heart (What)"

What have I done
I don't understand
You just won't kiss me
You won't hold my hand
What have I done
Been together all these years
You won't even look at me
I can't fight the tears

You don't have to sneak around
It's so obvious even the kid knows
We've been in motions such a long time
Even the color is gone from our rainbow
I can see where and when is my blame
Why don't you own up to yours
You haven't touched me for months
Looks like you're never coming back for more

Why do you go through with this
Instead of just letting go
I understand it's for our kid
Why don't you just say so
But give me this one question
And I guess I'll move on from this
What have I done to you
That it's been months since a kiss

What are we going to do now
What will get us through
Are we going to live this charade
It's really been all you
What are you going to say
When all is decided and done
What habits of mine upset you
That you took away all of our fun

Do you have a voice in there?
Do you even have a heart?
What is it saying to you
Are we finally splitting apart
Open up to me please
And let's get to the finish line
How shall we proceed now
Or are we another loss in time

What have I done
I don't understand
You just won't kiss me
You won't hold my hand
What have I done
Been together all these years
You won't even look at me
I can't fight the tears

I'm at my wit's end
What have I done
What have I done
What...have...I...done...

"Voices of the Heart (Why)"

Bluebirds are whistling
As the day evolves into noon
I'm sitting in tears
Flooded in my room
Don't understand the what
Don't understand the why
All I hear are these voices
Through all the tears I cry

Gave it my best efforts
The howling winds seem to agree
But as a storm erupts on the horizon
The skies seem to cry in jubilee
Assume correct as questions why
Why did he do that and this
Why did he cheat and then leave
Why am I alone and why not dismiss

Can't just let go of the past
Our lives are made up of things done
And while the rain beats on my roof
Just can't help but relive some
But these voices I can't seem to shake
Yesterday the what and today the why
So dominating in daily thoughts now
Painful like piercings in my eyes

Never find the answers I'm told
And eventually maybe I won't care
That these voices of the heart
Want to repeat and share
I'd give in but am so afraid
Of what these voices may say
Need the strength of a friend
To lean on for today

Squirrels are joyfully playing
As the storm rides by
My tears have dried up
As I put behind the whys
Don't understand the what
Don't understand the why
But I've got so much ahead of me
Can't afford to give up and die...

"VOICES OF THE HEART (LISTEN)"

Rain crackling on the trees outside
Signals a raw morning dead ahead
The autumn branches shedding leaves
Pushes a thought of an old girlfriend
Wasn't long ago we shared incredible times
Was a moment ago she left for good
But as the rain beat down upon my head
I wouldn't ask her back if I could...

As the moisture soaks into my sweatshirt
And the thought tries to stay prominent
I take a long breath in and sigh
And smile for my new found freedom
There's so much to be happy about
Even though the smile shines over a loss
For what's ahead is a dawning of newness
A discovery that will bring growth and love...

In this time of dampness and dreams
How can I know that such positives lurk
Again I smile and chuckle to myself
It's all in the voices of the heart
Just step back and take a deep breath
And listen to the voices of the heart
Give it undivided attention and find
Never go wrong listening to the voices...
   ...voices of the heart...

She's long gone as I chuckle again
Heading inside to the warm confines
Suddenly overcome with emotion
I perch myself at the kitchen table
Grasping a warm cup of tea and honey
Trying to shake the deep chills of rain
Stare off to the distance known as thought
And confidence sleighs any dragons mane

Another smirk from my parallel universe
I slurp down what's left and stretch
Reaching for the high heavens of life
And grabbing that golden ring warmth
I close my eyes in my silent solitude
Smile once more and whisper to myself
Such a beautiful day when you listen
Listen to the voices of the heart...

"Rainbow"

slow down
and grasp the day
hello ya got to say
cruising around the neighborhood
looking for an elusive rainbow...

breathe in
and feel the sun
gotta have some daily fun
searching for some buried treasure
looking for an elusive rainbow...

        don't need no promises
        don't need no rainy clouds
        give me a neighborly smile
        being up is all that's allowed...

breathe out
and heed the time
gotta relax what's in the mind
catching up on some needy pleasure
looking for an elusive rainbow...

slow down
enjoy the night
gotta do what feels so right
scoping out the feelings so good
looking for an elusive rainbow...

        ha...got one...

"Nerve and Effect"

twisted in knots so tightly
and stuck in current position
send out the emergency squads
for all the backbiting impositions
living in reality so composed
with a great deal of fiction
leadership so amiss amid stars
can't see results from friction

thoughts and nerves so intertwined
outlooks become so skewed
cross that invisible line in mind
and people have you screwed
the effects always affect outcomes
to the point of demotivation and then
the passion switches toward another target
until sanity previous comes to an end

      skewed visions
      misinterpretations
      erroneous decisions
      demotivations

      open the eyes
      see what is real
      adjust and realize
      seal the deal

"Dirty Mind"

Have a partner
A partner in time
A special someone
A someone in crime
Who has an obsession
Not necessarily mine
So uncontrollable
That dirty mind...

I'm full of innocence
A smile and a wink
But one look at you
And I know what to think
Don't have that kind of passion
To think this all the time
How does one control
Your perpetually dirty mind...

Have given in to you
Time and again
Each moment a new fantasy
Never seems to end
Don't have the energy
To keep up with you
Creativity and vision
How can I continue...
We make a great couple
We're a real exciting team
But I can't keep the pace
With all those dreams
It's time to recharge
Because I'm going blind
Dealing with your needs
And your dirty mind...

"GIVE ME THE TIME"

see starts in your eyes
and hope in your touch
with direction to the future
the excitement is too much
see your mind at work
every word just a tease
so playful and fun
can't wait to please

    though at times i sense
    a distance so far
    a stare so burning
    then a fading star
    i wonder what keeps us
    apart and why
    and what it would take
    to reach you and try

such a strong want
such an intense yearn
desire you to reach out
so we both could learn
the reward is euphoria
at least in my mind
and i'll gladly share
if you give me the time

    give me the time
    give me the time
    give me the time

see stars in your eyes
and hope in your touch
i'm in a holding pattern
with feelings and such
wish you'd get serious
and address the issue
let's move forward
and couple me and you

"Christmas Sits At My Window"

Christmas sits at my window
And peers out on a timely basis
At some moments admiring the frost
At some moments noting the time lost
      yet is ever present...

Christmas sits at my window
And surveys the surrounding atmosphere
At some moments postures sturdy and strong
At some moments limps willowness so wrong
      yet is ever present...

Christmas sits at my window
And stares off into the radiant distance
At some moments laughing and giving
At some moments struggling to be living
      yet is ever present...

      over the years
      sprinkled with love and tears
      families are home
      some folks families alone
      spread some joy
      make smiles Christmas toys...

Christmas sits at my window
And looks over the feelings of the heart
At some moments it's pure cold
At some moments warmth of the soul
      yet is ever present...

"Euphoria"

Read the word
Create the vision
Sense the ecstasy
Feel the power

    Say the word
    Hear the word
    Sense the phonetics
    Feel the tongue taste

Think the word
Envision the word
Sense the emotions
Feel the juices

    Dream the word
    See the word
    Sense the surreal
    Feel the reality

Live the word
Breathe the word
Sense the doings
Feel the life

"CREATION: CARING"

Walking through a sunflower field
Hand in hand our intentions real
Flight of butterfly no reason no rhyme
Watch it float with no sense of time
Fatal attraction we call this a team
Beacon of love that's set on high beams

   ...can't keep my mind from reflecting in time...
   ...dreaming and caring for you in mind...
   ...so focused on us though distance we share...
   ...hard for me to show you how much I care...
   ...hope you comprehend what I'm trying to write...
   ...that I'm so happy with you in my life...

With our distance we stroll hand in hand
Can't get over walking through this love-land
Follow the rainbow to this pot of gold
So wondrous that we share our love starved souls
No more stresses as we discover our bliss
After touch I know we can never miss

   ...can't keep my mind from reflecting in time...
   ...dreaming and caring for you in mind...
   ...so focused on us though distance we share...
   ...hard for me to show you how much I care...
   ...hope you comprehend what I'm trying to write...
   ...that I'm so happy with you in my life...

On the wings of a fairy's delight
Can't escape the emotional limelight
Any closer and we'll mold into one

Wish I could be there to share in some fun
There's no sensations that compare to this
Close my eyes and dream of you that I miss

  ...can't keep my mind from reflecting in time...
  ...dreaming and caring for you in mind...
  ...so focused on us though distance we share...
  ...hard for me to show you how much I care...
  ...hope you comprehend what I'm trying to write...
  ...that I'm so happy with you in my life...

"Who's Turn?"

Life goes into hiding
    as a punishing snow
        pummels the paths...

Nature winces emotionally
    enduring fierce winds
        and grounding all in its way...

Occupied mindless of past
    reflections of moments frozen
        dancing in oblique space...

A snuggle...
    a purr...
        a relaxing moan...

Who shall put
    another log
        on the fire?

"ABSOLUTELY NOTHING"

There's so much that life has to offer
So much love and life that fulfill us daily
So much hope and dreams that encourage
Yet why so much that brings us to fail thee...

Bring good news and experiences of the day
To nothing more than rolled eyes and a sigh
What has brought us canyons apart like this
Relationships and the hereafter faucets of cry...

   Absolutely nothing
   This is what I get
   Absolutely nothing
   No doubts or regrets...

The yearn of an equal existence pulls deeply
Though symbols of a deaf mute ring true
What does the meaning of this ring bring
What does life as one do for someone like you...

   Absolutely nothing
   No emotions to deal
   Absolutely nothing
   Finite end to seal...

"SOMEONE LOST A LIFE TONIGHT"

When I think about just last night
   muggy sights
     the dust jumping from the curtains hanging in there...
     just an experience that no one could care
And it's one more call and I don't hear you anymore
Who cares of struggles lately
We're all out there protesting like never before...

Someone lost a life tonight
   was a beacon oh so bright
     a mind of brilliance and a heart in flight
Tied and bound and kryptonized
Took the tour and hypnotized
Drew some freedom but lost some soul
Soared through life then lost control
Someone lost a life tonight...

Never realized the cursing power
   of lonely showers
     hanging threads on wistful wanton dreams...
     just a pawn in your everyday wild scenes
When the time is right, it's togetherness again
Don't hinder the soloness tonight
It's frozen in mind to be thawed now and then...

Someone lost a life tonight
   was a beacon oh so bright
     a mind of brilliance and a heart in flight
Tied and bound and kryptonized
Took the tour and hypnotized
Drew some freedom but lost some soul
Soared through life then lost control
Someone lost a life tonight...

Would do anything to feel you shiver
Give my life to swim in your river
Feel all numb until you quiver
Grasp any moment just to hold you
Breathe some life intensely into
Trade my life for you to continue...
    bleed for me... (pump those veins)
    seed for me... (grow life sane)
    wake up with this... (kiss)
    don't dare miss... (kiss)
    don't dare miss... (kiss)

Someone lost a life tonight
    was a beacon oh so bright
    a mind of brilliance and a heart in flight
Tied and bound and kryptonized
Took the tour and hypnotized
Drew some freedom but lost some soul
Soared through life then lost control
Someone lost a life tonight...

    Goodnight... (kiss)
    Goodbye... (kiss)

"In The Dark Again"

Thought we had a date tonight
    sometime after work
You tease yet not please
    and who feels like the jerk
You got me all up
    with a potential rendezvous
But I lie here in depression
    'cause this date is missing you...
    it's missing you...

I've been lying in the dark
Anger split me apart
I wouldn't of cared, thought business as usual, but it was you...
    you...YOU...who made this move...
I'm still lying in the dark
Depression from the start
I should have known it'd be a repeat of the past...
    but I'm a romantic and it ever lasts...
    yeah...the feeling ever lasts...

This is two nights in a row
    where you promised with a flirt
Now I lie hear in the dark again
    and look who is hurt...again who is hurt
It's been a challenging time
    a rough patch in our lives
But I thought we were gonna score
    I needed you oh so badly tonight...
    badly tonight...

I should have known it would end like this
But I needed your kiss
The timing's off now, too depressed to care

but then we both know that love ain't fair...
I should have known I'd be alone in time
But you know I am blind
I just realize that I'm not first...
    just lying in the dark again hurt...
    yeah, lying in the dark hurt...again

I'm lying here for hours
    waiting up for you
With a hope, a wish, a dream
    that we'll rendezvous
But I guess the time has come
    as the scars cut more deep
That any possibility has come and gone
    and it's time for us to sleep...
    time for us to sleep...

I've been lying in the dark
Anger split me apart
I wouldn't of cared, thought business as usual, but it was you...
    you...YOU...who made this move...
I'm still lying in the dark
Depression from the start
I should have known it'd be a repeat of the past...
    but I'm a romantic and it ever lasts...
    yeah...the feeling ever lasts...

Now sleep oh depressed one...
Now sleep oh angered one...
What to do with this feeling of love...
File it under the term 'done'...
    file it under the term...
    'done'.

"CRY FOR ME"

Such a beautiful brunette with the pretty eyes
Living a life full of challenges and tries
With a mission in mind and hope this day
That all the frustrations will soon go away...
    Life is not easy, life is not fair
    We pay for the past everyday, everywhere
    Take a moment, and take a stand
    Learn to give in and reach for my hand...
        and cry for me...

So overwhelmed with daily fears and distress
Sometimes burdened by lonely tears and stress
So thankful for the family and friends help received
Yet wishing that these issues would end and leave...
    Life is not easy, life is not fair
    It's the present we must focus and care
    Take a moment, and again be strong
    Taking time for yourself is in no way wrong...
        and cry for me...

    we in no way know each other
    we in no way have spent time
    but now i reach in prayer and hope
    your surroundings ease your state of mind
    and smile again...and smile again...
    lean on a new-found friend...
    cry for me...
    so you can smile again...

"Heart"

whole heart
half heart
pieces of the heart

encompass the emotions
warm the cockles
pick up the spirit
actually feel the warmth

unleash some passion
cage some rage
emote some fury
let go of the hostility

let depression escape
don't dwell on the sadness
wander through the grieving
don't turn anything into madness

pieces of the heart
half heart
whole heart

"Only So Many Pieces"

A yearning for honesty and integrity displays character
A driven passion to be able to spend time together
The alone time only progresses the interaction of mind
Especially when one feels that two should be one forever...

    Time goes...
    Time wastes...
    Time shows...
    Patience...
    It's passion...
    It's yearning...
    In fashion...
    Heart's burning...

The mind plays terrible tricks in perspective perception
Why one needs constant reassurance is a question
When two active people share a bond so iron strong
No doubts needed as only love should be the lesson...

    Believe...
    Feel...
    Proceed...
    Real...

Careful, for their are only so many pieces
In mind, body, heart, and soul...
Don't let emotions go too far
Don't let perceptions get out of control...

"THINK LINKS"

Need think links
Everyone here needs some think links
Raise a toast to some tropical drinks
Ohio blizzards and chills always stink
Sanity running to the brink
Someone keep me from going insane
Add some warmth, subtract the pain...

Need think links
Someone bring me some more think links
Gotta create before my dreams shrink
Not time to go it alone
So let's get this party sent home
Throw on some Buffett and let's play
Take all them winter blues away...

Need think links
Gotta research some more think links
Don't need any of you rat finks
Just fun folks who want to play
Mindset is not up for sway
Keep it simple and keep it fun
Plan to laugh awhile, the night's young...

Think links...
How I love those think links...

"ALL TIMED OUT"

Wake up alone on another morning
Outside it's a chilly snowstorm warning
Inside it's worse frigid weather
Whatever happened to being together
Thought there were some promises made
All that's left now is a bad charade

Don't you know I churn inside with tears
There's no place to turn and hide those fears
The quiet is so noisy in this dreary scene
You have escaped with all of our dreams
My acid tears are burning the pillows
Your spine so jelly go swim with the willows
I've cried and cried and cried no doubt
Now there's nothing left...I'm all timed out
    and over you...

There's nothing more that can be said
We've been squandered and left for dead
You were the one who wanted us first
Now I'm the one that's left with the thirst
Guess there's no more hidden treasures
I'm over being the one to give pleasures

I can't believe I gave all my love to you
Now there's no point to continue
I gave you all of my love in vain
Come here and let me give you my pain
Figures you can't even show your face
Your memory's faded now...been completely erased
I've cried and cried and cried no doubt
Now there's nothing left...I'm all timed out
        and over you...

        ...silly for me believing...
        ...that you wouldn't be leaving...
        ...silly for me to love you...
        ...silly for me to trust too...
        ...no more tears no doubt...
        ...i'm all timed out...
        ...over you...

"Forgive The Unforgiven"

Boy and girl meet one day
Both take each other's breath away
Quickly enhanced relationship brings
Sudden love and progressive things
As time moves on they see
It just wasn't meant to be
Much too late to calm the wild
She's already staggered with child

What they've felt and what they've known
Never displayed in what's been shown
They jumped through time and massive change
Now they reap the rewards of pain
They didn't see it could never be
Though stubborn they weakened easily
They took each other on way too quick
Eroded with problems too many too thick
　　　...now they're both unforgiven...

The child takes on a life from them
It's shuttering from unacceptance of friends
There's no time in this life to enjoy
Inherited pain so he grows up a bitter boy
And the spiral just continues to spin down
The rebel dominates the underground
And lives a life of hatred and doubt
Just can't figure what it should be about...

What he's felt and what he's known
Never displayed in what's been shown
He jumped through time and massive change

Now he reaps the rewards of pain
He didn't see...it could never be
Though stubborn he weakened easily
He took his lot too seriously
Eroded life he hurts unmercifully
　　　...now he's unforgiven...

There's a culture like all of them
Part of society that is all hurting...
Their lives handed down from generations
All filled with a strangeness in reverberations...
Just takes one with patience and time
To fix each of this unique set of mind
Cleanse the mind, evict the emotions cold
Warm the heart and live shall the soul...

What could be felt and what could be known
Could be displayed in what could be shown
All through time, effort and change
And leave behind all of the pain
They could see it could very well be
When open, it can be taken seriously
Give them a smile, give them a chance
And their lives could be a fairy tale romance...
　　　...now forgive the unforgiven...
　　　...now forgive the unforgiven...

"Passing Strangers"

We met one night as two youngsters so vain
Who danced in the dark and played in the rain
We had nothing but time on our side
We had everything that hope couldn't hide
    Passing strangers...

We met one night while playfully out
Eyes crossed each and gone was any doubt
Frozen moments from across a room
Time moved so quickly and ended too soon
    Passing strangers...

        Friends quickly whisper...
        Telling secrets and all...
        What's the next move...
        Don't stumble and fall...

We met one night and stood alone
Spoke of memories and moments unknown
Lust in our eyes and yearning in our souls
We were two passing strangers out of control
    Passing strangers...

We met one night by clutching emotions
The distance of feelings spanning oceans
The passion overwhelming we held on too tight
Dreams turned to dust eroded by sunlight
    Passing strangers...

"Visions of Red"

Captured face in a window of the night
Caught peeking through a beacon of light
Symbolized ashes of us still aglow
Let's burn passion now and forget tomorrow...
All these pictures left us for dead
All I can say is intense visions of red

Now read while the poems still remain
Relive the love and feel the constant pain
Promises made in silence yet still return
Forget the present and let those passions burn...
All these signs just point toward dead
All I can see is intense visions of red

See your friends faces as they glimpse by
Misunderstood and broken in their replies
Our breath appears in mist to hide the view
Forget what they see now it's only me and you...
All these friends had left us for dead
All I can feel is intense visions of red...

"Misty Dreams"

We walked in the frigid air
Freezing breath hung heavy out there
    cold stings full of pain...
Barely see through a window pane
Just two lovers in a picture frame
    caught in frozen rain...
A piercing cry from a house next door
Brings hopes of hearing no more
    as shattered was the mood...
This mystery proved way too loud
Suddenly we're back in a crowd
    both shivering as nudes...

    our feelings have left
    it's only you and i
    and these metaphoric scenes
    metaphoric scenes...
    of misty dreams...

We continued our distant walk
And turned up the volume of our silent talk
    though there was nothing to say...
Quickly standing alone in the night
Tears crystallized in the neon lights
    and just got into our ways...
Stretched to understand the silence
And two hearts that reeked of distance
    answers were there to see...
What became of the warmth of your hands
As we struggled again to understand
    the answers became clear to me...

our feelings have left
it's only you and i
and these metaphoric scenes
metaphoric scenes...
of misty dreams...

ACKNOWLEDGEMENTS...

This book is dedicated to everyone who can relate to any of these experiences printed in the preceding pages.

Illustrations by: Mike Haszto Jr. and Mitch Haszto.
Cover Design by: Jen Haszto
Thank yous go to:

    To Joyce and the kids, for helping to create the environment
    To lifeafterdark, for stimulating the creating
    To MAL, FLL, and CK73 for motivation in creation.
    To Professor Whippenpoof, for incredible vision

    To OHH for hockey fun every Friday, releases the stress!
    To The Jersey Club

Look for Mike Haszto's other book:
    "Of Dampness and Dreams"

Look for Mike Haszto's forthcoming novel:
    "Radio Frec Mickey" due at the end of 2008.

About the Author

Mike Haszto
Long Island NY native (hometown: Islip)
Now resides in North Ridgeville, Ohio

Writer/poet.

First book published, "Of Dampness and Dreams" is book of poetry generally based on life's experiences through the eyes of two unnamed characters. Second book of poetry "Pieces Of The Heart", (First book with AuthorHouse) is a collection of life's experiences depicting detailed emotions.

First novel, "Radio Free Mickey" is almost complete as well. It is the story of a mom and pop radio station owner, one of the last of its kind in the industry.

Avid fan of baseball, hockey, soccer. Hobbies include the radio industry.

Still plays hockey and indoor soccer in adult leagues.

Local high school hockey coach, youth hockey coach 17 years.

Parrothead disciple.

Favorite quote on writing...

"Anyone can write, but not many can express. The challenge of poetry is in creating the vision, then finding the right words to express it. I have written for over thirty years and find this to be the most challenging form of communication, and yet the most satisfying."

-Mike Haszto

Printed in the United States
128702LV00009B/172/P